Success from the Waist Up:

VIRTUAL MEETING

AND

PRESENTATION HANDBOOK

Judith Rasband AICI CIM

To order additional copies of this book, contact:
Xlibris
844-714-8691
www.Xlibris.com
Orders@Xlibris.com

ISBN: Softcover   978-1-6698-7489-8
         EBook   978-1-6698-7488-1

Print information available on the last page

Rev. date: 04/24/2023

Success from the Waist Up:

VIRTUAL MEETING

AND

PRESENTATION HANDBOOK

How to Make a Positive First and Lasting Impression on Zoom

Table of Contents

CHAPTER 1

Introduction

Traditional business meetings, presentations, conferences, and conventions will endure as a primary part of the business environment. The power and passion of real-world experiences and face-to-face interaction is still the most effective way to connect, relate, collaborate, and bond with others in business. Nonetheless, for many, the global coronavirus pandemic has required us to shift to virtual channels to meet our communication needs. Be it a business call, meeting with team members, connecting with clients, networking with new acquaintances, a webinar, or a live-streamed conference, we may do it online through Zoom. Zoom is the new conference room, with the host and participants attending remotely through video connections. Other platforms with similar features include Skype®, WebEx®, GoToMeeting™, © FaceTime, Microsoft Teams®, Google Hangouts™ and even more sophisticated platforms fit for different purposes.

Whether you or your workforce are back in your office or still working from home, this new technology offers us the amazing opportunity to connect with anybody, anywhere in the world,

at any time. I can speak at conferences without going there. It is a proven way to build stronger relationships with top people in our field and boost our productivity. But as our world becomes more virtual day by day, we are radically changing the way others see us and our companies. We need to look and sound as good as possible. We need to work harder than ever to increase our impact, influence, and income. We all have to become stars of our own show—on the computer screen.

While most of our most popular and profitable events were previously in-person events, we have been forced to quickly transition, to take what we once did in-person and transfer it into a digital format. Our virtual remote environment, self-presentation, and self-branding matter every bit as much or more than ever but come with a new set of unique challenges to be conquered. It is therefore essential that we get onboard FAST and sharpen our virtual presentation skills NOW!

The parallels between traditional one-on-one meetings or presentations in person and virtual or remote on-screen events are familiar and comfortable to some but may panic others. Success strategies typically determine whether virtual events are magical or mediocre.

Knowing the following strategies and tips for efficient and effective video communication, such as avoiding distractions, technical glitches and miscommunication, can help control 'video anxiety' or 'video phobia.'

Attention in this publication focuses first on environmental and technical preparations followed by content and slide preparation. Relevant topics that are generally not covered in other publications relate to self-presentation, including details about dress, grooming, body language, speaking, and stress management.

This manual serves as a guide for you as producer, presenter, and participant. It becomes an engagement-driven learning experience, enabling all to develop a professional, yet standardized performance so that clients will experience and come to expect the same level of attention, professionalism, efficiency, consistency, and courtesy from you and your colleagues each time they connect. Said competency will be positively noticed and valued regarding branding efforts as well as affect bottom-line results. Read the sections that interest you; then file the book for future reference when you realize that all the sections are all important.

CHAPTER 2
Planning the Event

Virtual events serve to take the place of in-person events, to be planned exclusively for on-line participants. Be it a virtual meeting or virtual conference, you need to think ahead and develop an intelligent, solid, proactive plan for success. You must prepare the people expected to attend. Set their expectations, why they are asked to attend, when, and where. Planning allows you to build in more interaction and participation.

I was a participant in a recent virtual presentation, primed to arrive on time, pay attention, and increase my knowledge of the topic. The presenter was late — 2 minutes, 5 minutes, 10 minutes late. Worse, he presented himself with bedhead and a rumpled shirt. He wasn't prepared. Supposedly he had to download some software and pick up new lighting. No amount of excuses saved the day and he never recovered. It was a virtual disaster.

When planned, prepared, and practiced effectively, virtual meetings, presentations, and conferences can be as effective and productive as live events, ensuring that you communicate effectively. They allow you to bring together participants separated by geography and strengthen relationships. They are going to revolutionize the workplace.

In addition, virtual meetings generally take less time, less labor, and cost less as well. The ability to display names on the screen does wonders to avoid embarrassment if you forget someone's name. Being guilty of this again and again, I love seeing those names. It's like everyone has on a nametag. Terrific!

Event planners are now more equipped to put on q virtual event than ever before. Nonetheless, your technology and tools are only as good as your ability to use them. Just assume some of your technology will fail. If you prepare, practice, practice, practice according to your plans, and keep your cool, your virtual presentation should be a success. Amazing!

Defining the Event

As you begin to plan your event, consider whether a virtual meeting is the best setting. You should only meet virtually regarding important topics that benefit from a collaborative discussion. Deal with more routine topics in a phone call or email.

Once you decide to hold a virtual event, it is time to consider the "who, what, when, where, how, and why."

Why Are You Holding the Event, the Meeting?

A successful meeting always starts with an important reason or strong purpose—the "why" of the meeting. Then move on to setting goals. Only after you have established the goals of the meeting, can you begin to consider who you will invite and what content you will cover. When defining goals, consider the following:

- What do you hope to gain by holding the meeting?

- What skills or information do you want the participants to gain from their attendance?

What is the Content?

Once you have your goals defined, you can start thinking about the path to meet the goals; this will help you define your content. I will write more specifically about content later but begin with the type of meeting you plan to hold. There are many types of meetings, such as an office or team meeting, a networking event, a brainstorming event, a webinar, or conference. This will affect the timing and audience of your event.

When Will You Hold the Meeting?

The timing and length of the meeting may differ based on the type of event. It is, however, smart to shorten all your meetings by 10 to 15 minutes, allowing a short break between meetings. We all need a break.

Office Meetings

Office meetings generally run from 30-60 minutes depending on the purpose and goals to be accomplished. In addition, you may want to limit it to eight participants, so everyone has the opportunity to speak and interact.

Office meetings should be in the morning hours. Because virtual meetings encourage bringing together attendees from different geographical areas you should consider the time zones involved when setting the time for the meeting

Networking Events

Networking events should be limited to four to eight participants to ensure that they have adequate time to interact and get to know each other. If they are previously unknown to each other, send an email to the group in advance with the name and a short bio of each attendee.

Webinars

Webinars are all about education, generally open to a larger audience and should occur in the afternoon. Once again, be sure to consider relative time zones in setting the time. Like office meetings, webinars should run 30-90 minutes. Because of the larger numbers of participants, these events tend to be much less collaborative with the interaction limited to the chat option within your webinar tool.

Conferences

Conferences are complete events composed of multiple sessions over 1 to 3 days. Sessions may or may not be run simultaneously throughout the conference. Attendance goals need to be set. Sponsorships may be an option to support the event.

Who Will You Invite?

The content of successful meetings is always driven by your goals and the audience you intend to invite. You should only invite participants who can actively contribute, collaborate and, most importantly, benefit from attending. Take a minute to review your goals as you create your attendee list. Individual contributors, managers, vice-presidents, whoever, will influence your content and the language you will use.

Virtual Meetings by Device

The mere fact that you are sharing information via a virtual platform like Zoom, does not guarantee that you can control *how* your participants will view the content. With so many device options nowadays, people could potentially attend your meeting via:

- Computer
- Ipad/Kindle
- Phone (Android or Apple)
- Smart Television

Platforms such as WebEx, Zoom, and Skype have adapted nicely in the past few years to render their content cleanly on any device that participants choose to use. Since you will be leading meetings with participants who could potentially be using one or more of the aforementioned devices, it is good to test what they will be seeing, and to plan your presentation accordingly.

Security and International Considerations

For security sake, it is always recommended that you use a password for your meetings. Zoom has made progress to plug up security breaches that were detected earlier. Static URL for Zoom Rooms, or Personal Rooms are good for informal team meetings and such, but not recommended for professional meetings and trainings. Always embed a password.

When presenting internationally, it is a good idea to contact the participants in advance to make sure that they are allowed to use Zoom. I have had many experiences where people were attending from behind a company firewall and were not allowed to use Zoom. On several occasions training European clients, I had to leverage WebEx due to their company policies. In Hong Kong I had to use Skype for Business for the same reasons. My most extreme example was once when I was training for a large automotive customer who had attendees from all over the world. I had 2 computers: one running Zoom and one running Skype. Fortunately, I knew this ahead of time. Don't just assume that everyone has access to Zoom, always be ready with a "Plan B."

Key Performance Indicators

Virtual events make it easier to capture data and insights including registrations, attendance, audience engagement, average time viewing content, and so on. These key performance indicators (KPIs) help you know where to invest your time, efforts, and resources, allowing you to achieve any marketing and sales goals. Your platform of choice needs to enable you to track this data.

Many virtual attendees want to rewatch content from events they've attended. This should be considered as an indicator of event success.

Invitations

Once you have your list of attendees, you need to prepare the event invitations. It is likely that you are inviting busy people so plan to send the invitations well in advance to increase the likelihood that they can attend. Be intentional about every detail.

- Segment event invitations for different audiences according to interest. A sales executive may want to attend for one reason while a new hire might be attending for some other reason. Personalize the value propositions according to role and goal.

- The invitation should include the day, date and time of the event. Identify the different time zones involved and print them in sync on the invitation.

- State the goals for the meeting: why you are meeting, the key talking points, what you intend to accomplish, what your expectations are for the participants.

- Sharpen your event titles and descriptions.

- Make the invitation engaging and compelling.

- You may include the link to the meeting in the video platform you plan to use. Some meeting hosts will choose to wait and send these once attendees have accepted the invitation.

Reminders

Follow-up your invitation with a reminder. Reminding those invited why the event might be valuable to them will refresh their memory and increase the likelihood of them attending. The reminder should include an agenda using section titles or headers with key talking points. Include a list of any documents or other items the participants need to bring to the meeting, letting them know that you will be calling on them for input.

Do not assume that all your meeting participants know how to dress for the event. Advise them to dress the part—looking like the consummate professional in their field, relaxed but professional.

- If preparation time is needed for a particular topic or question, assign it to a specific person.

- Let participants know they may join without video if they prefer or that you expect the camera to be on the entire time.

- Let them know if you will be recording and whether or not you plan to send them a replay.

Follow-Up

Building relationships among your people is strained in the remote environment. So, once the participants have accepted the invitation to attend, send the link to the meeting if you did not send it in the original invitation. This is the time to designate certain people to ask or answer specific questions during the meeting. You may also choose to send a list of participants with contact information if appropriate.

Email a "thank you" note within the day of acceptance, continuing to forge a positive relationship. The longer you wait, the less impact the gesture holds.

Send a professional headshot of yourself to the meeting host to be used as your screen image. If your video does not work properly for some reason, your photo will be available for any gallery view. Also, if you must move away from your screen as you present, you can simply click the video option off and turn it back on when you return. In the meantime, your professional photo communicates your presence. It is also your option if for any reason you would rather not be seen live on screen.

Planning For the Unexpected

Getting down to the nitty-gritty, many people had never even heard of "Zoom" before the Covid 19 pandemic hit. Now it's all around us, everywhere, and everyone is expected to have figured it out, including virtual event etiquette.

Whether you're a novice or a veteran, you learn that it's easy to lose your focus during a meeting. It's generally rude to multitask during a meeting. It's no time for a quick check of your email which can turn into fifteen minutes away from your event content.

Maintain apparent eye contact and smile whenever you pause, just like in person. Be sure to breathe deep and regularly to avoid getting light-headed or dizzy.

If you work from home, make sure every family member knows what you're up to, to stay out, maintain quiet, and to stay offline themselves.

Regardless of experience, we all live in fear that the technology won't work or the internet may go down. It happens to most of us at one time or another. Plan for a technical practice run prior to the meeting to confirm that they'll work when you're ready.

For those in charge of technology, be sure to have the information specific to this technology in advance. There are different types of virtual communications which unknowingly could sabotage the virtual event.

Click in a few minutes early to confirm connection and reliability by being on time. This also allows you to engage in some small talk with your group—to share your latest family news, travel news, a media story, even a recipe.

People will most likely have questions about some of the content as presented or discussed. It is rude and disruptive to interrupt or talk over someone to get a word in. Suggest they write down their questions on a post-it note to remember to ask at a more appropriate time, or use the chat function allowing you to submit your question silently.

Experience shows that seldom does a meeting start on time. Do not let this happen if at all possible. Again, it's rude to hold up the meeting, causing presenters to rush through their material, not cover all information, or run over-time themselves. It's smart to state in the invitation that you plan to start on time and end on time—then follow through.

If you know in advance that you have to leave a virtual meeting early, it is polite to notify your host. Have a professional headshot available to post as a back-up for such a time—or if you need to walk away for any reason. Remember to "mute" your microphone. Check back regarding any missed content.

For those totally unexpected moments that are beyond your control, don't be afraid to tell the truth—children or the dog bursting through the door, slides not sharing, lighting explodes—it happens. Just laugh, relax, acknowledge it and begin recovery. We can do this!

CHAPTER 3

Staging the Event

The environment you choose to host the event is a key component to your success. In this chapter I am going to focus on selecting the location and background, as well as preparing the technical aspects of the meeting, such as the lighting, camera, and sound components.

Location and Background

A video call is a window into where and how you live and work. Be it in your office or at home, you need to have the focus of your participants' attention in the center of the screen. Make it simple, neat, neutral, and devoid of distractions so that viewers can easily focus their attention on you. You may love fancy wallpaper, but it will compete with your face and what you have to say. Consider these best practices for a successful meeting:

- Avoid windows behind you. First, anything happening outside the window will be distracting. Also, the backlit glare will cast you as a dark silhouette.

- Avoid extreme colored backgrounds. A very dark background may appear to drain your personal coloring. A very bright background will visually dull your personal coloring.

- Position yourself in front of a plain wall. It's hard to go wrong with a plain softly colored or white wall, ideally 4-6 feet behind you allowing enough distance to show some depth. For some people, a plain wall relieves distraction.

- Pay attention to any wall art or decorations behind you because your audience certainly will. They need to be business appropriate to connect with this meeting, this audience. A landscape picture is generally appropriate, but avoid glass-framed art that will catch the light and create a glaring reflection.

- It may be smart to remove family and vacation photos, banners, awards, trophies, and/or flags. They can take too much attention to themselves—unless they are personal information you actually want to broadcast, allowing people to become more well acquainted with you. They are likely just fine when you are working from home, appearing less cold, sterile, and able to spark natural "small talk." For a conference, however, they take away from the professionalism of the event—and you need to be the center of attention.

- A bookcase background is popular, but make sure the book titles are appropriate if zoomed in on. Even then, audience members may be distracted by reading all the titles. It is smart to create a 50-50 split—books on one side of the shelf and decorative item on the other. Reverse the book-decoration layout on each shelf.

- You can replace decorative items with your company logo if it

does not compete for attention with your face on-screen. Standing or potted plants are also a pleasing replacement for personal items.

- If having a wall behind you is not possible, arrange visible furniture behind you in an orderly manner. Make sure there is no exercise equipment in the background.

- Consider a virtual background. Most platforms offer virtual backgrounds including the option of blurring the background, although a blurred background can be hard to focus on.

- Do not move too fast because the background may blur, or the edge of your image may flutter distractingly—the "bouncing head" effect.

- Avoid backgrounds not consistent with the integrity of your occasion or purpose. A photo of you in front of the Eiffel Tower, the Bay Bridge, a cityscape, or Hawaiian beach may be exciting or fun, but obviously fake and possibly distracting.

- With Zoom, you can upload images that can be branded to your company or association, or to the client's organization. If you choose to do so, you may need to have a greenscreen behind you to help deflect the glare. A greenscreen may also be needed so you avoid disappearing when you move.

- It may be smart to avoid a big talking head for hours or days on end. Do change background locations periodically for variety or visual style—even outside. Consider a scenic background relevant to your location. Photograph the scene and upload it to your background.

- Consider a scenic background relevant to your location. Photograph the scene and upload to your backgrounds.

Neat and Clean

Regardless of location, your surroundings are subject to scrutiny and say as much about you as the points you are making.

Any clutter or mess is distracting and will likely communicate a lack of organization and order in your business, as well as a lack of attention to detail. You may choose to live as you like, but your viewers do not need to see it all.

I remember well, meeting with a potential client in her home office where an unmade bed, bath towels, and underwear filled the space behind her. These are things I did not need to see. Set the stage properly for the occasion.

- Put away your pens, pencils, scissors, tape, stapler, and so on.

- Put your notes in a business binder.

- Arrange books neatly in the bookcase.

- Straighten any pictures or wall hangings.

- Remove any food or clothes lying around.
- Position a smaller glass or bottle of water nearby, no big bottles or jugs.

Looking Professional

Lighting

It is important to control the lighting for your event. Eliminate unwanted shadows on your face because faces are hard to see or focus on and may appear to alter your facial expressions, making you appear less trustworthy.

- Position yourself facing a window or position a light at eye-level behind the computer or camera you are facing. Better yet, set up two lights on either side of your monitor, about 3 feet apart, and level with your eyes.

- Lighting should be in front of you, shine directly on your face, making sure it is not so bright that it washes you out. It is also important to avoid light shining from the side, behind or above you which causes dark shadows. Turn off any overhead lights, because they will tend to make your eye sockets look like deep, dark holes. Back light from a window behind you makes you look like a dark silhouette. If possible, avoid fluorescent lights.

- If you wear glasses, look out for any glaring reflection of light. Many have seen ring lights reflected as demonic circles in people's glasses. If you notice a glare, it may help to tip your head slightly downward.

- The laptop or monitor will also light your face, so make sure the main light source in front of you is stronger. If you are conducting an important meeting or webinar, you should acquire a self-standing, dimmable ring light. These are reasonably priced and can solve a host of lighting problems. You may want to consider a pink light for a softer effect.

Camera

If using a desktop computer, you will need a webcam. Even expensive laptops may have low-quality webcams, so if your built-in laptop or computer camera does not meet your needs, consider investing in an external high-quality web camera. Webcams are available in a wide range of prices, including some very reasonable prices. A smart phone is generally fine for social contacts, and some of these cameras may be of higher quality than most webcams.

Camera distance and angle

Your camera must be positioned for a pleasing view of your face. Position yourself at a distance from the camera much like you would be if you were talking with someone face-to-face. You might prefer being an arm's length from the camera. Whichever you decide, do not get so close that your guests feel like you are 'in their face'. And don't forget to clean your camera lens frequently.

Framing

Position the camera just above your eye level, pointing just slightly downward. Don't have a lot of space above your head. Overhead lights and ceiling fans are distracting. The video feed should frame your head and shoulder area. You do not want to be looking down into the camera or have viewers look at your neck or up your nose for the entire call or meeting. Looking at an upwards angle to the camera can make you appear child-like. If your chair position is too low, try sitting on a bar stool to achieve eye level.

Elevation

Elevate the camera if necessary. Put your camera, laptop, or iPad level on a box, a stack of books, an ironing board, a stand, or tripod to raise it to the appropriate height. Make sure the computer or camera is level.

Sound

Sound quality greatly affects what your audience hears. If the sound quality prevents participants from hearing you properly, they will log off immediately and your meeting or presentation will be unsuccessful.

For most events you can rely on your built-in computer microphone. However, If the built-in computer mic does not meet your needs, consider using a clip-on lavalier mic, or dedicated microphone like the Blue Snowball. These are readily available at a reasonable price and may vastly improve the quality of your audio.

Prior to the Event

Before your meeting, you will want to properly test your sound setup to ensure great quality.

- Make sure you've got a strong Wi-Fi connection.

- Make sure the microphone is plugged into your device and properly transmitting audio.

- Test and adjust the volume settings using the device's sound settings.

- If you find that sound quality is an issue that you are not able to resolve, pre-record the session. The speaker can answer questions live after the presentation.

During the Event

- Speak relatively close to the microphone. Then maintain your distance from the microphone. Moving around will result in inconsistent volume and possible distortion.

- Use headphones only when you need to eliminate outside noise or to enhance hearing. Headsets with cups over your ears or earbuds tend to be visually distracting. Video calls or chats seem more natural without these devices. Another option is hidden earphones with a built-in microphone.

- Mute your microphone whenever you are not speaking to avoid unexpected noise or necessary outside conversation. Background noise disrupts your meeting or presentation.

- If you are using Zoom, rely on the "Mute upon entry" option to ensure that your participants join with their sound off. When it is your turn to talk, do not forget to unmute yourself. The "unmute" can also indicate that you're ready to contribute, signaling to group members to give you the opportunity to be heard.

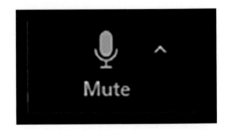

- You should know how to take questions from the audience using the chat option or Q&A tool. The polling option is another tool to consider using to make the session more engaging and interactive.

- Ensure that your audience is familiar with the interactive tools and can use them effectively.

CHAPTER 4
Developing the Content

All the technology and tools in the world are useless if you have nothing to say. In theory, your content is what brought your participants to your presentation in the first place; Your content is key to keeping them with you for the duration. Winging it is not an option. Make your content positive, productive, and profitable!

Participant Satisfaction

Every bit as important as when presenting in person, you must plan, design, and write your content for your event audience well in advance of the event. If at all unsure about the content, create a pre-event survey to learn what your audience wants. Then deliver exactly that.

Be very aware of the words you use. Words have meaning, convey mood, evoke emotion, and signal action. Use words appropriate to your profession or purpose. If unique to your profession, define them. They will establish you as an expert.

The Opening

In theory, your opening and closing are the most important parts of your presentation. Begin with an opening statement that asserts WHAT you are meeting for and WHY. Make clear what your purpose or goal is and the message you wish to convey for the meeting, webinar, or other event. As you introduce what you are going to tell them, if possible and appropriate, continue this in story form. The introduction must preview and lead naturally into the body of your presentation.

The Body

The body of the content is all of your related and supporting content. Tell them the whole story in chronological order as you progress through your content, but don't front-load your content—putting all your best "stuff" first. Break the body of your content into chunks, alternating with the related story or activity to maintain participant engagement. Space your best "stuff" throughout the body of your program to engage your viewer and avoid Zoom fatigue. People tend to speak for too long a time, rather than editing the message down to its main points. You can number the points within your message, helping your audience to stay on track and attentive. Save a S.T.A.R. moment for last—**S**omething **T**hey'll **A**lways **R**emember!

The Closing

As you wrap up, you have the opportunity to review and relate what you have covered to the goals that you set out in your opening. Review what you told them, again in story form, emphasizing the solution or results. Close or conclude with a call to action. It must be exciting, logical, and doable.

Q & A

Depending on the type, purpose and topic of the meeting, give some thought to Q & A periods. A good Q & A period can move you into a personal exchange that people love. You can also space short periods of Q & A throughout the body of your program, specific to the topic. You can tell a great story relating to the question.

Scientific and medical presentations need to rely on questions at the end. Some experts advise to never close with Q & A. You give up your final minutes to others, risk awkward silence, or end weak, not knowing an answer. Maintain control by asking, "What questions about what we've covered do you have for me?" If there are no questions, say "I must have done a great job."

Perfecting the Presentation

Complete a first draft of your presentation. Make sure that you include everything you want to say.

Next, work through a second draft defining how you want to say it.

Then, finalize a third draft where you edit everything for grammar, punctuation, and clarity.

Practice, Practice, Practice

Once you have the content finalized, the next step is to practice, practice, practice out loud until you own it.

- Visualize yourself presenting your message.

- Video tape yourself giving your presentation.

- Practice in front of a mirror.

In reality, attendees are not buying your content. They are buying your performance or delivery of your content. Determine how to make it better. Then do it!

Preparation for the Event

Prepare any participant materials and use them to speak from, memorizing the content as necessary. Get the participant material prepared to distribute by email when you are ready for the participants to have them. Make up a set of note cards to use if needed. You will look more prepared and will sound more conversational if you use them.

Experience and research confirm that it is more difficult to educate or influence virtually, remotely. Trust tends to be reduced and skepticism increases in a virtual environment. We tend to be less likely to believe, more likely to disagree, and harder to convince or persuade when meeting virtually. We have got our work cut out for us. Why is it so hard? Because you are competing with your participants' daily life, especially if they are working or attending from home. At any moment, they may be distracted by the dog, a crying child, the mailman, a neighbor knocking at their door, or focused on something else completely. No one will be the wiser. If you are not constantly engaging with your audience, you will not know if you have lost them.

Hosts and speakers benefit by positive support from participants during in-person meetings—like applause and even cheers. Missing from virtual meetings and events, it's still important to show support and encouragement. Get yourself into the chat window with positive words of encouragement or to literally cheer people on. Meeting planners have been known to supply all participants with a set of pom poms to be shaken vigorously in place of applause.

Stimulating Slide Show

In a webinar or conference presentation, participants tend to lose attention after about 10 to 20 minutes of listening to the same presenter. Many participants are visual learners, so bring your content to life and keep your viewers on track with a selection of related, relevant slides or encapsulated within a well-designed PowerPoint presentation.

- Use classic or corporate branded type fonts, colors, and logo that are easily legible. Consider how the fonts look across the variety of devices.

- Stimulate viewers' attention with intuitive pictures of real people and data relevant to your topic. Use one slide for each concept or specific message.

- Keep your slides simple with fewer words and graphics that serve to explain your message clearly. Avoid using animation. You can fill in with details as part of your spoken presentation.

- Print minimal text on each slide, presented in virtual "sound bites" — short statements that explain the picture and relate to your message.

- Create purposeful slide titles or headers to inform the viewer about the main message in the slide. This helps viewers better follow along. Consider using a little alliteration, rhyming, or an oxymoron to catch attention. Keep a thesaurus and related dictionaries handy.

- Include some white space around the title, picture or text box, allowing the slide to appear less jumbled. Too much detail competes with the message you are trying to communicate.

- Avoid staying on one slide for too long. Move right along to maintain interest. If appropriate, invite different people to present a slide or two. This serves to engage your audience. Address the person by name.

- While you do not want to induce slide hypnosis, there is no agreement as to whether you should use more slides or fewer slides as compared to an in-person presentation. Regardless, when using slides, your face is reduced to a postage stamp in the corner of the screen. This is the time to power up your voice to better hold the audience's attention.

- Do not overwhelm viewers with endless charts and data causing them to zone out. Put the slides up, then take them down, connecting with the audience again.

- Resist the advice to send your presentation notes and/or slides to participants prior to the meeting. If they have all that, why bother attending? Send them in advance only when participants must learn about something, ponder something, come up with questions, or come to some solution or decision prior to the meeting. Even so, save something to be a surprise, a S.T.A.R. moment — **S**omething **T**hey'll **A**lways **R**emember.

- Your technology and tools are only as good as your ability to use them. If the virtual event is more than a call or a chat, drill yourself with the platform you are using, becoming able to easily make adjustments if something goes wrong. Do the same with your background, lighting, camera, sound, and slides or PowerPoint. A technical backup plan is always smart—a designated co-host to take over if needed.

- If you are the host of the event and are at all unsure of your ability to handle the technology, I highly recommend you assign or hire someone to be on hand to takeover if needed.

- Make sure all participants have the device essential to receive your presentation and that they know how to use it. Encourage them to download and test the meeting software prior to the event

- If some technology fails during your presentation and cannot be corrected, do not belabor the awkwardness of the situation. Simply reschedule and later e-mail the update.

Virtual Conference Events

A virtual conference is a major online event dedicated to one main topic or concept, featuring multiple sessions, speakers, and experiences or activities. Covid 19 has propelled us into an era of hosting virtual conferences much faster than we were prepared for. Planned conferences were canceled and those with time to adjust had to quickly adapt and switch them to a virtual format. If you want or need to produce and host a riveting virtual conference, give thought to the platform you are using.

You must first protect your conference from "zoom bombers" — hackers, and internet trolls who crash your event, interrupting with crude and obscene, or racist comments and images you can't escape from, usually resulting in the shutdown of your session. This widespread exposure to hackers demands a secure registration platform with passwords. You must also ensure that the ID code is not shown in the title bar during the session.

If you are in charge of producing a 1-3 day virtual conference, you will already have your hands full. The last thing you need is to be the primary technician as well. Hire an experienced support person to oversee and run the entire event. You may also appreciate engaging an emcee, social host, or moderator to open the event, to open and close each session, and to moderate questions for the speaker. Having a second face and voice adds interest and can promote familiarity and consistency among all the sessions. It's smart to have a few questions prepared in case questions from the audience are slow in coming in.

Conference speakers have likely attended, and/or presented at a previous online event and will think they are relatively prepared for your event. However, because every online event software platform is different, you must make sure that your speakers are very familiar with the platform you will be using. Stories abound of presenters who were caught off guard when their expectations did not match a particular platform. Some presenters for example may depend on their notes being "hidden" during presentation. If the notes are not available, they panic. This is a good reason to always have a printed copy of your presentation content with you, including both slides and text.

At an in-person conference, things happen. You may make a surprising connection with someone or become involved in an amazing discussion that goes on late into the night. Life-changing things happen at a live conference just by virtue of being there. In virtual conferences, however, you have to make things happen. You have to make the experience more engaging and more memorable by including relevant interactive exercises or activities periodically—brainstorming, chats, polling, video clips, Q&A, and more to come.

I say periodic activities or exercises because recommendations I have received regarding the time between speaking and activity varies from 2 to 20 minutes. A lot depends on how good a speaker you are. Nonetheless, the rule should state, "Use activities or exercises only when they add value for the participants."

Activities for Lively, Engaging Events

Consider these best practices for keeping your conference lively, engaging, and FUN.

- **Illustration & Demonstrations** — Research and bring in pre-recorded content relevant to the session topic. Pre-record your own content to illustrate, demonstrate, or clarify important concepts that are impossible to present in a virtual session.

- **Break-out Sessions** — In Zoom, with a pro account or better, you can separate into small groups for a short discussion. You can appoint discussion leaders ahead of time so they can become prepared for their topic.

- **Use Polls** — Enliven the experience periodically with a poll. You can ask single choice, multiple choice, or open-ended questions to measure participant knowledge at intervals throughout the session. Give reward points and tally at the end of the conference for a certification of some significant sort.

- **Use Surveys** — Put out a survey for participant response. Use a survey to collect feedback about the event, measure participant learning or just as a checkpoint to see how participants are engaging with you.

- **Kahoot** — Another great way to engage your audience is with a word game or a short quiz. Kahoot is a free, fun, and interactive way to quiz participants.

- **Card Sorts** — Create card sorts relevant to your topic. Putting cards in participants hands engages the tactile and the visual learner.

- **Lunch Breakouts** — At lunch breakouts you can invite participants to share recent articles they have found relating to your topics. Participants can choose which breakout group to attend based on the topic.

- **Share Experiences** — If you want participants to become more well acquainted, use lunch breakouts to invite them to show something that has special meaning to them. It might be a wall arrangement of family generation photos, a relaxing garden location, a well-loved pet, whatever. Make it fun!

- **Gift Bags** — This takes time and requires postage, but it is a favorite because everyone loves receiving a gift. Well in advance of the conference, solicit sponsors to provide small products for gift bags or boxes — things like hand lotion or sanitizer, breath mints, a tissue packet, a to-do list pad, a travel toothbrush and toothpaste, or a chocolate bar. For my Retreat groups, I include in their gift bag a Utah Truffle Bar made locally, including a mail-order form. At every break time, invite participants to reach into their gift bag and pull out a surprise.

When carried out well, experience confirms that participants love these activities. They want to clap to applaud your efforts. But since we cannot hear the applause, I resort to my high school days as a cheerleader. Send all conference participants a single six-inch pom-pom in company or association colors to shake wildly when enthusiastic about commending the speaker.

Mix Live and Pre-recorded Content

In planning a conference, consider a hybrid approach to speaker presentations — as a simu-live event. Pre-record each of the presentations, edit and replay it at the conference as if they were live sessions. This allows each speaker the opportunity to deliver a more perfect presentation. If they make a mistake, just re-record and re-edit until they get it right. Then, located in the virtual event platform during the playback of the presentation at the conference, each speaker can answer questions and chat with their audience while the presentation is going on. Plan for 10-15 minutes of questions after the playback, with the speaker live on camera. This tends to personalize the experience for participants.

Another point of personalization... at the end of each in-person meeting or conference session, participants look forward to a little networking time—likely in the hallway. At the end of a virtual meeting or conference session, participants have no such interaction with other attendees. So make time, five to ten extra minutes more on Zoom at the end of each session—a sort of hallway space for conversation and networking.

Schedule 15-30 minute breaks between speaker sessions. Participants will appreciate time to move, stretch, tend to family, eat something, and/or use the bathroom. At the same time, you can solve speaker or technical issues that might have come up.

Before closing a conference session, make sure you put out a call-to-action that provides follow-up steps for participants. This might require reading, writing, or action regarding the topic of the session, later the conference as a whole.

Follow up with a post-conference satisfaction survey form. While the virtual conference is still fresh in their mind, find out how satisfied they were with their experience. Provide options for participants who attend a single session and for participants who attended multiple sessions.

CHAPTER 5
Projecting your Image

Delivery skills are often lacking or magnified in virtual meetings and events. Yet you can develop your delivery skills as you learn and apply the following content. Another word for appearance is image. Being looked at as a leader, your image is as important as your content. Knowing how to present yourself appropriately, authentically, and attractively serves to set yourself apart from others, signals that you are capable, credible, and trustworthy.

Deliver a Dynamic Virtual Image

Your clothing or dress is the first Element of Image, covering the largest area of your appearance. It is a non-verbal visual communicator. Your viewers perceive you first through your appearance, your self-presentation before you say a word. Your appearance affects your message and how it is perceived. Remember, you are on camera. Because the camera is always on, operating virtually means we are, you are always on, too.

Dress with intent. Match the mood and the occasion. Some people think that a virtual meeting or video conference does not demand the same level of professionalism that an in-person meeting does. Others know this is a mistake. When participants are visible, each may look at others more closely on screen than they do in person. While no one expects you to show up in a formal three-piece suit, you can't afford to look as though you just rolled out of bed or off the treadmill when you connect virtually. You need to look as if you are focused on the business at hand. This calls for a little social-psychology to maintain your on-camera clout. It's a sign of respect for the other person, for the occasion in that you really did put effort into yourself, prepared to speak with them.

If presenting a webinar or conference session with participants you do not already know, make it a point to learn about them. Dress for them to a degree. Do not dress down or you risk losing your visual authority as host or presenter. If you are the presenter, your audience may look up to you as the expert in your field. Dress the part, to look like the expert — smart, sharp, organized, ready to increase their knowledge.

Understand this, the way you look affects the way you think, the way you feel, the way you act, and the way others react or respond to you. It is much the same whether you meet in person or on screen. When you look better, you will think and feel better — with more energy, interest, and confidence. You will act better — sit or stand taller and speak stronger with more enthusiasm and ability! As a result, giving the people you're meeting with visual cues or clues as to who you are, your viewers will perceive you as better — more credible, confident, capable, and productive — as a leader. It works!

Dress up to Power Up

Because you are only a virtual image on a screen, it is easy to become overly relaxed. Are you showing up to a planning meeting wearing pajamas, workout clothes, an old t-shirt, boxers, shorts or sweats, a baseball cap, and flip-flops? Remember, how you show up on screen matters just as much as how you show up in person. Intentionally, show respect for yourself, your peers, your company, and for the occasion by looking professional from head to toe. It sets you up to behave like a professional. Show up looking somewhat relaxed, but still commanding visual authority and attention before you say a word. If the event is a team effort, discuss dress as part of your preparation. You are all on camera.

You never know if or when you will have reason to stand up, so don't assume viewers will see only your face and shoulders on screen. The story is circulating about one woman who reported showing up for an online conference with her lower half undressed due to spilling coffee on her lap just before the meeting started. Looking professional from the waist up, she was perfectly fine in her panties until the mini cam fell off her computer. Jumping up to get it, her team got more than they bargained for—a little TMI. It becomes a topic for a tweet.

Just as with your location and background, nothing in your outfit should distract attention away from your face — nothing fussy or that you have to fuss with. Clothing style lines and shapes that are extreme, in bright colors, bulky fabrics and/or busy patterns distract attention away from your face. They become the center of attention, diminishing your presence, visual authority, and influence on camera.

Clothes Communicate

Tailored classics — timeless clothes designed with simple straight lines and angular shapes — increase your visual authority and influence. No cutesy "girlie" styles with puff sleeves and ruffle necklines for women.

Style Line & Shape

Focus on your top. Rely on button-front shirts with a straight or spread collar. The straight lines communicate "alert." The diagonal lines communicate "action." The collar works to draw attention upward and frame your face for better communication. Do not wear rounded Peter-Pan collars as they lose visual authority. Ladies, if you wear off-the-shoulder tops you may look naked on camera. That's certainly one way to compromise your credibility.

A third layer adds visual authority and is terrific when you need or want it. Consider a lightweight shirt-jac, vest, sweater, duster, or jacket. A relaxed looking blazer or sport jacket is always an option. Men, if wearing a polo shirt, layer it with a sport jacket. A classy tie, suspenders, or a scarf can work as a third layer and draw attention up to your face. Look through your closet, catalogs, or local stores. You will find some great options to add a layer of credibility and grace to your message.

ColorSense

Do not wear clothing the color of the wall behind you. A blue shirt in front of a blue wall and you will look like a floating head—distracting. To avoid blending into the background, wear a contrasting color. You want to set yourself apart from the background. If the background color is light, wear something darker. If the background color is dark, wear something lighter. You have a wide range of options.

Rely on "wardrobe neutral" colors — slightly muted, rich hues. The camera loves you in complementary contrast colors — blues, purples, and greens including teal blue green. You will look terrific in analogous reds, burgundy, and coral. Rich brown, olive, and charcoal gray or muted rust also work well. All of these colors repeat and/or contrast handsomely with personal coloring.

Darker "wardrobe neutral" colors tend to appear more visually authoritative, while medium to lighter colors appear more approachable. Stay away from shocking pink, neon orange, or chartreuse which can be overpowering or appear threatening. Wear black if it makes you feel fabulous. Large amounts of pale pastels, white, or light gray will reflect a lot of light and appear to wash you out. Avoid taupe, as seen on the left, a dull grayed-brown color, unless it matches your hair perfectly and is offset from the background.

Choose to wear one solid color providing higher contrast for more visual attention, as described above. Or a combination of dark and lighter color. Examples include navy and white, black and ivory or shrimp, hunter green and light blue, brown and red or pink, cinnamon and teal, camel and charcoal. Again, when it comes to color schemes, you have many options. Repeating your hair, eye, and blush colors is always a great choice.

Low contrast   High contrast   V neck increases visual authority

Fabric & Texture

Choose medium to lightweight fabrics and textures. Heavy, thick, bulky fabrics add visual weight to your body, especially on camera. Smooth, tight weaves and knits cause you to appear more visually authoritative, while textured, looser weaves and knits cause you to appear more approachable. Lightweight fabrics work for layering relaxed looks in warm to hot weather.

Pattern Savvy

Choose more subtle patterns, ideally designed to include your hair and/ or eye color, making you part of the color scheme with your clothes. Angular patterns tend to appear more authoritative, while rounded patterns appear more approachable. Avoid large, strong, or busy patterns and no faces, slogans, logos, salamanders, or baby bunnies. They take too much attention to themselves and weaken your influence. Avoid narrow stripes and zig-zag patterns as they appear to vibrate on camera. Tattoos are distracting patterns. Cover them so your message can come across.

Accessories

A well-coordinated scarf and medium scale jewelry are smart and add visual interest. Too much jewelry or jewelry that is very large becomes distracting. Small to medium size earrings work to hold attention up around your face. Stay away from swingy, dangling, or tasseled earrings and noisy bracelets.

Wear a real pair of shoes. Flip-flops and sneakers are tempting as it is not likely viewers will see your shoes. Nonetheless, shoes with a solid sole will support you better. You feel more confident and sit or stand taller.

Make sure your clothes are clean and in good repair. Wrinkles, thread snags, food stains, and ring-around-the-collar do show up on camera.

For additional clothing standards and styling, see *Fabulous Fit,* by Rasband.

Fit to Be Seen

All clothing should be comfortable to wear. Comfort is a matter of fit. Maintain your professional image and comfort with clothing that fits your body. Fit is the number one complaint from consumers about ready-to-wear clothing. Just because you can get into the clothes does not mean they fit. Attention to detail adds to your credibility and comfort.

- Clothes should be sized in scale with your body frame or bone structure. Everyone can wear medium scale design details, making it a relatively safe selection for all. Wear clothes that fit you NOW—don't wait on your weight to buy the clothes that you need NOW.

- Clothes that are too big with loose vertical folds can make you look like a clown — dumpy or frumpy. They may be comfortable, but they work to drag attention down.

- Clothes that are too small with tight horizontal or diagonal wrinkles make you look stuffed in. The viewer's attention is drawn to wherever the wrinkles form. And they are uncomfortable.

- For a comfortable fit, you need to be able to slip one or two fingers easily inside your neckline and waistline without pulling or stretching.

- Basic shoulder seamlines need to line up with your shoulder joint. On clothes made with shoulder pads, the shoulder seamline should extend beyond your shoulder joint about ½ to 1 inch. Think of moderate shoulder pads as fitting tools, not fashion trends.

- With your arms hanging down at your sides, long sleeves need to be hemmed at the top curve of your thumb. When your arms are bent upward as they may be on screen, the sleeve hemline will rise to your wrist bone, exactly where it should be. Too short or too long both appear silly and uninformed. Short sleeves need to cover your bicep.

- Give yourself the "pinch 'n inch" test. At chest level and low hip level, you need to be able to pinch ½ to 1 inch of ease front and back — extra fabric allowing you to move and the fabric to slip easily over your body without pulling or stretching. Buttons and pockets should never gap or pull open. No "boobalicious" views!

- For a dress slim effect, a center-front row of buttons, a zipper, a longer necklace or tie, and lightweight layers in contrasting colors work to create a strong vertical line that draws visual attention inward. They also lead attention up to your face.

- Tuck shirts into your skirt or pants with about an inch of ease or "blousing", unless designed otherwise. Shirts tucked in communicate order and attention to detail.

For complete fitting standards, see *Fabulous Fit*, by Rasband.

Shop In Your Closet

Before thinking about the need to buy new clothes for Zoom, shop in your closet. Make time to put together several terrific outfits you can put on quick and easy, allowing you to feel more relaxed and ready to go online. Creating a positive impression will make you look and feel professional, in control, sharp! Then look a little longer. Maybe you have a top or a dress you haven't been wearing for awhile due to tight fit below the waist. Maybe it's too short below the waist. Maybe the style or fit above the waist works just fine, just right for Zoom calls. Hang these garments aside in your closet and consider them your Zoom outfits.

Grooming Detail

Grooming is the second Element of Image. It is another non-verbal, visual communicator. Good hygiene and grooming can eliminate more distractions and increase your visual authority. Studies reveal that facial preparedness will help you earn more money too.

- Both speaking and your delightful smile reveal your teeth. Teeth must be clean and in good repair. Salad on your teeth is distracting, to say the least. Never pick your teeth on camera.

- Natural looking makeup for women, used in moderation, can make you look more alert and healthier, smooth your complexion and add dark-light value contrast to increase attention to your face, particularly to your eyes for better communication. Blush makes your eyes look brighter and lipstick makes your teeth look brighter. Make sure there are no noticeable layers of foundation, no baby-doll circles or streaks of blush, no bright blue, pink, yellow, or purple eye shadow, no exaggerated wings with eyeliner, and no bright pink, orange, blue, or black lipstick.

- When appropriate, men benefit from a little powder or powder-foundation to even skin coloration or cover a shiny nose, forehead, or bald head. Try a little bronzer to avoid appearing washed out. Men also benefit by wearing moisturizer, having a clean-shaven face or neatly trimmed beard. You do not want scruff creating shadows on your face.

- Your hands may be in the picture. They need to be clean, smooth, well-manicured, and non-distracting. Use clear or natural nail polish color to maintain attention on your face. Avoid nail polish in black, brown, purple, green, blue, and yellow when on camera.

- Your hair is your "crowning glory", so it is said. Clean and neat are a must and definitely no "bed head." Oily hair needs washing; dry hair needs a little oil applied after washing. Hair coloring needs to be natural or natural looking, in harmony with your personal coloring and clothing. Your hair frames your face. A balanced hairstyle works to hold attention on your face.

Before   After

- Spiked, scraggly, or straggly hair draws attention away from your face. Hair covering your eyes makes you appear untrustworthy. Continually brushing hair out of your eyes is distracting. Long hair can draw too much attention to itself and appear to drag you down. You can style it back or in an up-do. If worn long, let one side hang in front, but position your hair on the other side behind your shoulder letting your clothes speak for themselves. Do not wear any messy buns or little topknots perched smack on top of your head.

- If a distracting grow-out is beginning to show, buy a liquid concealer at a beauty supply store. It is easy to apply directly on your hair without touching your scalp.

- To further enhance your appearance and feel camera ready, Zoom and other platforms include touch-up filters you simply click into. Check the Settings menu. They actually make you appear younger with smoother skin, fresher, and alert.

Body Language

Body language is the third Element of Image, a non-verbal visual communicator. Trust is usually developed in person through eye contact and body language. This is still true on screen. Body language speaks loud and clear, before you even say a word. Enhance your image with expressive, effective body language.

The appearance of eye contact is as important on screen as in person. Make sure your audience can see your eyes. You want them to feel a personal connection— like you recognize they are present. It helps to think of the camera as the person you are talking to.

I still remember a goofy virtual meeting I attended. I say goofy because the presenter stared down at the screen or off to one side the entire meeting. I wondered where his mind was. What was so interesting "over there"? It was actually quite distracting.

- Get your body where it needs to be ON TIME!

- Posture is noticed first. Even though your viewers can generally see only your upper body, your shoulders are a key communicator. Slumped shoulders say you are tired, sad, less alert, and lacking confidence. Viewers may see you as less trustworthy, with less ability. With your shoulders back, you take deeper breaths and tend to look slimmer, healthier, alert, attentive, and interested. Your voice will also be stronger and more direct.

- If you are going to be sitting for a long while, put a pillow behind your back to aid you in sitting tall. Keep both feet on the floor. No crossing your legs. You will feel and appear more alert, confident, and capable—an expert in your field. No rocking on your chair. You might really fall over.

- Look straight into the camera lens when you are speaking, not at the screen. Look at the person you are speaking to. Look at the face of others when they are speaking. Resist the urge to look at yourself on screen. Do not squint or stare at your notes, the floor, or ceiling.

- In presentation mode, have a little fun. Give your viewers the opportunity to smile, laugh, and connect. Smile as often as appropriate for your topic. It adds a sparkle to your eyes. You do not want a non-stop grin, but a genuine smile connects and warms the heart of everyone. It's your best accessory.

- A smiley face sticker is a great tool to put on the camera lens. It gives you someone to talk to.

- As in a typical conversation, make your hand gestures and head and shoulder movements deliberate, purposeful, and meaningful. Gestures punctuate your words and provide a natural release of nervous energy. The more you use your head, hands, arms, and body, the more your voice will sound energized and confident. Nonetheless, slow down your gestures to avoid looking frenetic and do not gesture too close to the camera or they will look humongous. Virtual video is a close-up medium, so make your gestures small to medium or they get lost beyond camera view. Ladies, adjusting bra straps may be purposeful, but we do not need to be made aware of the problem.

- Turn your head to the side to cough, sneeze, or yawn—away from the camera to take care of the issue.

- Do not make nervous gestures, like fussing with your scarf, glasses, hair, mouth, nose, ear, pen, or pencil which betray anxiety. Avoid scratching your head, biting your fingernails, cracking your knuckles, twisting a ring, or doodling. Your hands belong in a resting position or quietly on the table or desk. You can also rest your forearms on the edge of the table, indicating that you are "aboveboard" or trustworthy, not "underhanded." It is appropriate to rest your chin on your hands when in thought. Tilt your head slightly to show interest, or nod in agreement.

- No eating when on camera. Drink from a straw in your glass or small bottle to prevent viewers from looking up your nose. Better yet, turn your head to the side when you take a drink. No snacking.

- Resist the urge to multitask when attending a virtual meeting. Do not mix paid work with housework. Do not read a magazine, your e-mail or check your snail mail, and again, no eating. This tends to reduce your attention, adds to your stress, and increases mistakes and productivity. Add to that, other participants notice that you are not fully present.

- When you are making a specific presentation or report on Zoom, adjust the camera position or location and stand up if location allows. Stand balanced on both feet with shoulders back and head held high. You will be able to breathe deeply, you will speak more clearly, with more energy, and vocal variety. Use a podium if you like, but no distracting logo or words should be on the front of the podium.

- To avoid video phobia, practice speaking on camera. The more you practice speaking, the sooner you'll start feeling more comfortable on camera. Consider recording a few meetings to watch yourself later. We all make our share of "bloopers," but catching yourself in the act can help us get over them. I want you to love seeing yourself on camera. I want you to feel confident, knowing that you've mastered looking terrific through your dress, grooming, and body language. I want you to be able to attract, engage, and enchant your audience for the total of your time before the camera! You can do this!

CHAPTER 6
Conducting the Event

Speak Your Piece

Confirm your non-verbal, visual Elements of Image with effective vocal or verbal communication. This qualifies as a fourth Element of Image. Your visual and verbal messages must match or agree! You cannot appear one way and act or speak another. Words are powerful; they define us. They can be remembered and recalled — some words you can never take back. The words you put out will come back to you, so choose your words carefully. Use your visual image as a resource to support and reinforce your spoken words. Speech becomes a matter of etiquette as you interact with others through greetings, conversation, and collaboration. Remember or refer to names on a shared screen and use them when you direct a comment or question to someone.

- Speak in shorter sound bites to be more easily understood. Master the power of the pause. Pause after each important phrase or point, allowing your audience to process what you just said and fix it in their mind.

- Conscious voice control is required to create the vocal variety needed to engage and hold participants' interest. This includes varying your tonal quality, volume, pitch, speed, and degree of enthusiasm as appropriate to match your content. Speak at moderate speed and volume but be very careful to avoid speaking in a monotone. Also, avoid ending a statement with a question in your voice or trailing off at the end of a sentence.

- The need to enunciate clearly with no mumbling or slurring of words cannot be overstated. Increase your vocal energy to communicate passion, conviction, or emphasize a point. It can feel a little uncomfortable at first, but with time will become second nature.

- Speak using correct grammar and pronunciation. Do not use slang, profane, vulgar, sexist, or racist words. Stay away from acronyms. Avoid clutter words or stammering, such as ah-h-h, um-m-m, and-uh, like, or well. Also, you should not use modifiers like 'sort of', 'kind of, maybe or hopeful. They make you sound uneasy and uncertain. Repetitive or trendy junk words or phrases, such as neat, cool, like, sweet, awesome, shut up, etc., will diminish your credibility and authority.

- Position your print material as high and close to the camera lens as possible, allowing you to read at eye-level so your eyes and head do not slant downward as you speak.

- When presenting, direct your comments to "you" rather than to "everyone." Your viewers will feel you are speaking directly to them individually, rather than to the masses. If you are speaking to your team or associates, use the word "we" as often as appropriate.

- Listen when others are speaking and respect their input. Do not interrupt but wait for a pause before speaking. Be as positive as possible, giving genuine comments and compliments, while avoiding complaining or criticizing. Virtual tools are dependent on internet transmission speed on both sides of the conversation. Be aware of the possibility of a transmission delay after you speak. Pause, allowing time for the other person to respond.

- Avoid apologetic greetings, unwarranted or excessive apologies, nervous giggling, and finishing the sentences of others. Do express your appreciation, letting participants know you value their input. All the while you are reading their facial expressions and body language to ensure that they remain engaged. Be prepared to interject one of your activities or use a question if you sense their attention is wandering.

- Be very conscious about not getting off-track or straying from your agenda. A relevant side comment or story is fine but get right back to where you were on your agenda. If you get hijacked by a strong personality or negativity from a participant, stand and exclaim, "Interesting, but getting back to the agenda..."

- Ask questions when purposeful. Use closed questions to assess engagement or agreement. Use open-ended questions to open up a discussion. Do not hesitate to call on people by name.

- Discourage cross-talking among participants unless absolutely necessary. Then, make sure to mute your mic.

- When you are stressed or tired, your mouth can get dry and cause your tongue to stick to your teeth making it difficult to speak. Arm yourself with tiny lozenges, such  as Chipurnoi Puntini cinnamon candies, which can be ordered through Amazon. They last for ages whether soft or hard. Before speaking, put one down in the corner of your mouth to the side of your tongue. The tiny lozenge can stimulate saliva in your mouth while it melts for about 30 minutes. No one knows it is there. And no, I've never accidentally spit one out while speaking.

- If you get distracted, forget your lines, or your next point, come up with a way to get them back. Maybe it is a quick look at the handout or a strip of colored post-it notes. My favorite way is to ask my viewers, "OK, get me back to where I was," and I literally lean back or walk a few steps back to where I was. Nearly always, a viewer will cue me in.

- If you start to bomb or bore your audience, do not speed up. Slow down, breathe deeply, and refer to one of your viewers in relation to your concept. That will get attention and show that you are aware of each participant. Then ask for questions if you like. Have a common question in mind that you can tell a tiny story about.

Stress Management

It is totally natural to feel self-conscious and uncomfortable when you begin using a video conferencing tool like Zoom. It is normal to be concerned about all the technology you have to control. Relax and give yourself time. The more often you use it, the more capable and confident you will become at communicating virtually. But if necessary, assign or hire someone to assist you well ahead of time.

Maintain your personal/professional image with the following guidelines.

- Invest in a quality chair built with lower-back support, and an ergonomic mouse and keyboard to reduce health issues.

- Be in place a few minutes ahead of time. You will feel relieved and more relaxed.

- Carry out a tech rehearsal before the event. Make it a practice to call to an associate and rehearse screen sharing. You will reduce your stress level simply by knowing that your Wi-Fi connection is strong and your computer or other device, camera, and sound are working together perfectly.

- Turn off all devices and competing software programs. Make sure windows are closed, ceiling fans are off to prevent flickering, and air conditioners are turned off to eliminate distracting noise.

- Alert others in the office or the house that you will be on a call. Escort any children and/or pets to another room and shut the door. Put a "Do Not Disturb" sign on your door. If absolutely necessary, lock the door by installing a doorknob that locks. You cannot afford to be interrupted during an important event, so arrange for a sitter or nanny for the time period. However, do not come unglued if a dog barks or a child pops in during your session; stuff happens. Stay loose and keep your cool.

- Log into the meeting about 10 minutes early, to test the technology. Take a last look at your agenda and make sure you are ready to go.

- When your virtual meeting is not a scheduled webinar or conference, start with 4-5 minutes of more relaxed social banter. Everyone needs to connect personally periodically. "What's new with you?" is an easy opener.

- Maintain a positive, optimistic attitude even when you may not be feeling it. Use positive self-talk to create your own mindset and boost your confidence. We can become that which we speak so eliminate the negative thoughts and smile even when you are downright depressed, fearful, or angry. And never take yourself so seriously that you cannot laugh at yourself!

- If you're engaged in conversation, slow the conversation down. Don't think you have to explain or justify every point. Don't let your emotions take over! Let the other person do the talking while you listen, giving you time to get the whole picture so you can formulate a good response. If you need to know more, ask questions.

- Mistakes happen to everybody — you mispronounce a word or a name, you say something dumb, you misspell something on a slide. Be prepared with a few witty one-liners so your viewers recognize that you are human, that you are not upset, and are still in control. My favorite is, "Oh, you never do that, do you?" They have, of course, so you get a little chuckle and some empathy.

- Keep essential comb, hairbrush, makeup, and mirror near-by for a last-minute touch up before signing on. Having them handy is known to keep stress or anxiety levels low.

- Standing up periodically is a good move. It breaks monotony and allows your body to stretch. Sit, stand, sit, stand. Raise the screen accordingly.

- Apply the 20-20-20 routine. Most people have an attention span of about 20 minutes. So key into that. For every 20-minute presentation period, take a 20-second break and focus your eyes on something at least 20 feet away. This little routine works wonders.

- Practice the best relaxation technique on the planet. Take a big, deep breath and exhale slowly through your nose. You will literally feel the tension drain away.

Begin with a Bang

You are a representative of your business or company and therefore must present a positive, confident, and capable image. That means removing any last-minute distractions, being camera ready, and mentally prepared. If you are making a call or joining a chat, be ready with a positive greeting. Check the latest news for something current that relates to your conversation. If the virtual event is a meeting, a presentation or a seminar, engage your participants even before you begin.

• Create a virtual waiting room for your audience members to enter before you begin the session. Give them time to settle in, invite them to write down what they hope to get out of the meeting or presentation.

• Start ON TIME! If you are the host, you are responsible for opening remarks. Meet your participants' expectations and welcome them with ENTHUSIASM! Introduce yourself if necessary. Carry out appropriate guest or participant introductions. Recognize sponsors, senior participants, or dignitaries by name. Thank them for attending. If you like, invite a few individuals to share what they hope to get out of the meeting.

• Outline meeting expectations. If necessary, set any rules or guidelines and agreements for the hour or the day. With small groups, invite questions, comments, and feedback with a raised hand. With large webinar or conference groups, invite them to use the chat function. If you like, you can ask participants to mute themselves when not speaking.

• Announce any break time. If you are presenting remotely to a group in a conference center, you may have to identify restroom locations.

• Announce whether participants will receive a recorded play-back for review. If you plan to use the recording in the future, you must get permission from all participants. You may have to invite anyone wanting to decline, to sit out of camera range.

• Position the day's schedule nearby for reference. Transition speakers and topics in correct order, making names are perfectly pronounced.

• Yes, it can be distracting to see your own face front and center. Nonetheless, look directly into the camera lens to establish the appearance of having good eye contact with the person to whom you are speaking. Avoid looking at yourself on screen or it appears you are not looking at the individua or the audience in general.

- Then pause, looking into the camera. Exaggerate your opening statement with plenty of vocal energy, adding a question that demands they raise their hand in agreement. You already have them engaged!

How to Tackle Zoom Fatigue

It's clear that virtual meetings are part of our new normal, but if you are feeling drained by the end of a long video conference call or totally burned out by the end of the day, it's likely you are experiencing what is called "Zoom fatigue" and it's real! Stanford University scientists have confirmed that video meetings are more exhausting and stressful for participants than face-to-face meetings.

Why are video meetings so tiring?

- In order to appear like you are paying attention, you have to continually stare at the camera, contributing to eye strain and tension in your eyes. Add to that, you need to maintain continued eye-to-eye contact.

- In theory, seeing your own face on screen while talking can be both distracting and disconcerting. Having to stay centered in the camera's field of view leads to a feeling of being physically trapped.

- In a typical video call, you appear less than two feet apart, an uncomfortably intimate and intrusive distance.

- Virtually, meetings force you to focus more intently on the speaker's words or conversations just to take in all the content.

- It is easy to lose your focus due to surrounding distractions. Extended focus time may lead to boredom, indifference, apathy, and disengagement — a desire to just be quiet for a while.

- Having to sit still for long periods of time takes a toll. Aches and pain may develop in your neck and spine due to the way you are sitting.

Zoom fatigue is worse for women, who report feeling more exhausted than men following video calls and meetings. Researchers found this due to "self-focused attention"—a heightened awareness of how they come across or how they appear in a conversation—women being more apt to self-focus more than men when they are in the presence of a mirror. What researchers call "mirror anxiety." In addition, women's video calls tend to last longer, and women are less likely to take breaks between calls or meetings.

It would seem that the obvious answer to Zoom fatigue would be to turn the camera off! Not so. Wrong solution for this problem. By turning off our cameras, we make ourselves less interested, less informed, less impactful, and less influential. With our cameras off we appear to be doing something else. We appear disinterested, rapport becomes lower, skepticism and distrust become higher. Therefore, I advise turning your camera on for all virtual, remote meetings and events. Being able to see the impact of our communication on others is an incredibly powerful piece of information if we intend to modify, adapt, and increase our influence virtually.

Additional factors affecting tiredness include race, age, and personality. People of color reported a slightly higher level of Zoom fatigue compared with white participants. Younger individuals reported higher levels of tiredness compared to older survey participants. And introverts reported higher levels of exhaustion than extroverts. More anxious individuals reported more exhaustion than calm, emotionally stable people. Fascinating information to feed into solutions.

It helps to remember that Zoom and similar platforms do have their advantages, particularly getting people together safely and from long distances apart. But don't assume that someone will feel more comfortable during a virtual meeting because they're not in front of an in-person audience. It can be just as nerve-wracking to face a screen full of faces as it is to stare at a room full of actual people. So, what can we do to relieve anxiety, reduce exhaustion, and improve mental health?

- If possible, rely on a phone call or email for one-on-one conversations. Others may appreciate a break from video calls too. Rely on a phone call with people you do not know well.

- Implement no-video meeting days. If video is not necessary for a meeting, make it an audio call only.

- To keep your video call partner from virtually invading your personal space, set a default maximum head size—smaller. It works!

- As a participant, do not let yourself become distracted or ambivalent, thinking 'I don't need to listen to this, get involved with this, I really don't care about this'.

- Dress up to lift your mood and manner. Wear rich colored clothes to avoid monotony. Dress like you mean business on business calls!

- Plan shorter meetings — 25 minutes rather than 30, 30 minutes rather than 40, and 50 minutes rather than the usual 60.

- Plan for momentary breaks. Remember the 20-20-20 rule— every 20 minutes take that 20-second look 20-feet away from the screen, and engage in extra deep breathing to relax.

- Be sure to use breaks to stretch, to rotate your head and neck. It'll help you relax.

- Agree as a group that everyone will use a plain or simple background to reduce the distraction of background bookshelves, photographs, plants, etc.

- Agree as a group that everyone who is not talking will turn off your video for part of the call and listen only. Stand up and move around, bend and stretch.

- Stop looking at yourself, which is what most of us tend to do, if you are distracted by and obsessing over every little blemish or wrinkle.

- Stop multitasking. Shifting between tasks is taxing on your brain. You really cannot capture and hold the speaker's words in your memory while doing other things.

- Decline back-to-back invitations. Plan for more time between calls. 5 or 10 minutes between is not enough to relax and regroup.

- Make social sessions opt-in for all — welcome but not obligated to attend. You might put in an appearance but not stay for long.

It may take some time to put all these points into practice, but it is well worth avoiding becoming Zoomed out!

You should always look forward to the virtual event being over—big sigh of relief! It can actually become fun to send "thank you" notes as soon as possible—email within 24 hours. Waiting longer lessens the impact the gesture holds. Follow with a "real thank you" note, handwritten and mailed to reinforce your thanks and continue to forge a positive relationship for the future. You will instantly stand apart and show that you regard them as special to the success of the event.

CHAPTER 7

In Conclusion

History will record how quickly and abruptly Covid19 changed the world we live in. Zoom and similar platforms have proven to be effective alternatives for conducting business meetings, presentations, conferences, and events remotely. It is not likely that businesses will go back to pre-pandemic levels of in-person or in-office collaboration. Virtual is here to stay and part of the new normal. We will continue to adapt and with it, personal image will continue to be relevant to success in everyday life, in person and on screen. It pays to be "camera ready" at all times. As virtual meeting technologies evolve, the medium of presentations will also evolve.

Please do not think that because your event is not live, that it is not great. It is simply different and sparked with a vision for the future. As we master this technology, become skilled at virtual communication and remote interaction, let us remember to be extra kind, patient, and professional at all times. Remind yourself, that the way your preparation and presentation is seen on screen today affects how you will be remembered tomorrow—magical or mediocre. You need and can make a positive first and lasting impression to achieve your goals and make your vision a reality. With what you've learned in this handbook, ongoing preparation and practice will give you the ability to stand apart and succeed.

Printed in the United States
by Baker & Taylor Publisher Services

Be it a business call, team meetings, connecting with clients, networking, a webinar, or a livestreamed conference, we now do it online through Zoom or similar platforms. This technology enables us to connect with anybody, anywhere, at any time. It's a proven way to build relationships, save time and expense, and boost productivity. but comes with a new set of challenges. It is essential that we get onboard FAST, sharpen our presentation skills NOW!

This publication focuses on organizing the event including the who, what, when, where, and WHY for holding the meeting. Staging the event includes essentials about backgrounds, lighting, camera, and sound. Building the content, perfecting the presentation, and stimulating slide preparation follow. Attention to conference events embraces ways to engage participants. Relevant topics often not covered in other publications relate to self-presentation with details about dress, grooming, body language, speaking skills, and stress management. This handbook serves as a guide for you as participant, presenter, and producer.

Judith Rasband AICI CIM is a veteran university and international authority on visual design, wardrobing, and self-branding. CEO of the Conselle Institute of Image Management, Judith holds degrees in Family and Consumer Science. She is author, columnist, and speaker, trainer, consultant, and coach to private individuals, civic, corporate, government, and academic organizations and associations. She is a passionate consumer advocate. Students and clients appreciate her no-nonsense honesty and frankness, yet she's never so serious she can't laugh at herself and the sometimes hilarious reality of fashion and image consulting. An image industry icon recognized for her advancements in the field, Judith received the image industry's highest award, the "Immie" for education. Autor of the trusted Wardrobe Strategies Series and the Image Management Quick Reference Guide, Judith is cited for accuracy, innovation, practical applications, high-energy presentations, contagious enthusiasm, and lots of serious fun—landing her on Oprah, GMA and Today.

Xlibris

ISBN 978-1-6698-7489-
5189

The Harborside Inn

A history from 1914 to 1980 by Leo P. Convery